SELL THAT BOOK

WRITING ESSENTIALS BOOK 3

M.L. HUMPHREY

Copyright © 2018-2022 by M.L. Humphrey

ISBN 978-1-950902-88-0

All rights reserved.

No part of this book may be reproduced in any form or by any electronic or mechanical means, including information storage and retrieval systems, without written permission from the author, except for the use of brief quotations in a book review.

Previously published as *Achieve Writing Success* under ISBN 978-1722643439 and 978-1-950902-42-2. Also published under ISBN 978-1-950902-97-2.

ALSO BY M.L. HUMPHREY

Writing Essentials

Writing for Beginners

Excel for Writers

Data Analysis for Self-Publishers

Affinity Publisher for Self-Publishing

Affinity Publisher for Fiction Layouts

Affinity Publisher for Ad Creatives

Affinity Publisher for Basic Book Covers

Affinity Publisher for Non-Fiction

INTRODUCTION

I was originally going to write a book about self-publishing and some high-level topics that new self-publishers need to understand if they're going to either succeed at self-publishing or at least be happy with the outcome of their self-publishing efforts.

But as I wrote that book I realized that much of what I had to say applied to any new writer, not just self-publishers. Because, really, self-publishing and trade publishing are just two different paths to the same goal: being paid for what you write.

And so, whichever path you take, you are going to need to learn some of the same lessons. For example, that *what* you write will have a big impact on your success. And that if you fail to meet genre expectations you will suffer for it.

So this book is for newer writers, but not brand new writers. If you're brand new, check out *Writing for Beginners*. It's designed to ground you in what it means to be a writer. This book is for writers who have finished at least a novel but are not yet successfully published.

By successfully published I mean that you're making good money on your writing. If you're at that stage chances are you've probably already figured out the things I'm going to be talking about in this book. Intuitively if nothing else.

This is also not a craft book. I will touch on my developing theory on the different levels of writing ability, but this book is more business-oriented. It's for writers who want to sell that novel they wrote, either direct to readers with self-publishing or to a publisher with trade publishing.

Much of what I'll discuss here applies to non-fiction writers as well, but most of the focus will be on writers of commercial fiction (mystery, romance, speculative fiction, etc.) and on publishing full-length titles. (So I'm not going to be talking about writing for magazines or submitting short stories, for example.)

Now, who am I? What qualifies me to write this book?

I am a writer. Self-published at this point although ultimately I expect I'll pursue what's called hybrid publishing where you have some titles self-published and some titles trade published. I write non-fiction, mystery, romance, and fantasy.

At this point I've published over a hundred titles ranging in length from flash pieces to novels. Some have done well, some have not. I am more successful at this than many but much less successful than others.

I've been self-publishing for about eight years now

and over the course of those eight years I've listened and watched a lot.

Because I write such a variety of lengths and genres I have a broad range of personal experience with all of this, but I also have the benefit of years of absorbing the stories other writers have shared about their journey.

In my former day job I was a consultant who was paid very well to gather information, compile that information, form observations from what I'd gathered, and form conclusions about it. That's what I've done in this book. I've watched, I've learned, and now I'm sharing what I found.

If it helps convince you to listen to me, I also triple-majored at Stanford, have an MBA from Wharton, and attended the Taos Toolbox Writing Workshop. (Although none of those qualify me to write this book. It's my time spent absorbing this industry and personal experience with being a writer that matters.)

I think there's value to be had here. Whether you agree or not is up to you.

I will also warn the grammar purists right now that you will probably not like my writing style. I start sentences with "and" and "but" and I end them with prepositions. I use alright instead of all right. I also use fragments and ellipsis and parens. If all of that is like nails on a chalkboard for you, you probably don't want to read this book. (Although there's a lesson in the fact that I do what I do that you might learn if you read on...)

Okay, then. Enough of that. Let's get started.

THE PRIMARY DETERMINER OF YOUR SUCCESS

As I mentioned in the introduction, I am self-published. And in the early days I spent a lot of time on a writing forum where a lot of serious self-publishers hung out. (Which has since been ruined by new ownership.)

On a fairly routine basis someone would show up there and say, "My book isn't selling. Please help me. What have I done wrong?"

The responses were generally focused on three things: cover, blurb, and sometimes title. The cover isn't good enough to snag the attention of a busy reader. The blurb isn't enticing. The title makes no sense for the genre.

On rare occasions, and usually only when it was really obvious, there would be comments on the editing or the writing. Or maybe even the formatting. Or choice of category.

And while I agree that all of those factors are important in selling a book, they are not the most important factor.

The single-most important factor in how successful you are going to be as a writer is *what you write*. The more of a potential audience there is for your books, the more you're likely to sell.

Now, if you're like most of us, you already wrote something. You're sitting there with your precious manuscript that you now want to share with the world. You bled and cried to create this story. It is part of your soul. It took you years to write.

(I'm laying it on a little thick, I know.)

Well, I'm sorry to say this, but for most of you what you wrote is not going to sell well. It either won't attract publisher/agent interest, if that's the path you're on, or it won't attract a lot of readers if you self-publish.

You won't know for sure until you try—writers are horrible at judging their own work and life can sometimes be surprising—but chances are you didn't write a book that meets the needs of a hungry market. Not on your first try.

Many, many new writers delight in mashing up genres or blurring the lines of a genre. They think to themselves, "It's so boring how romances always end with the couple getting together. I'm going to write a romance where they don't get together. Or better yet, where the love interest turns out to be a serial killer!"

Or "Why do fantasy heroes have to always be these wide-eyed farm boys? I'm going to write a hero who is a jaded, old man who does crappy things all the time and refuses to save the world."

(I can't tell you how tempted I am just typing that to write that second story...)

Your novel may be fantastic. It may be brilliantly written. But if it isn't what your buyers are looking for (so agent/publisher for trade, readers for self) selling that book is going to be like pushing the proverbial rock up the hill.

If you write a book your buyers are looking for, it's like starting at the top of a hill and just having to push the rock off the side. Momentum will do the rest.

Let me talk about this from a self-publishing perspective first.

Readers don't go to Amazon and say, "Give me a book that's unlike anything I've ever read before." They go to Amazon and say, "I want more Stephen King. What do you have that will make me feel like I do when I read Stephen King?" Or "I want more Twilight. What do you have that's like Twilight?"

That's why you see so many book descriptions that say something like, "The Avengers meet Bridges of Madison County." (Not a good pairing, but you get my drift.)

Readers tend to want more of what they like. And the more you can give them "just like Stephen King" or "just like Twilight", with perhaps a small twist so it doesn't feel derivate, the easier it will be to sell your book. (Assuming there aren't eight million other authors also delivering books that meet that need. This is why a market can be a hot one in January and dead by December.)

When readers come looking for what you've written, it's a lot easier to make sales. (And therefore earn money.)

Now, this has nothing to do with your writing ability. If you publish a book that doesn't sell, that is not a reflection on your storytelling ability or your ability to write well. (It could be. That could be part of it. But the bigger issue is probably that you've written something not enough people want.)

Take this to heart now.

I repeat: It is not about your writing.

It is about what readers want and how much effort they're willing to put in to find what they like.

Don't despair if you haven't written something highly marketable. Just adjust your expectations. Know going in that if you wrote a literary novel about the ennui of middle age that you're going to have a harder time getting sales than that person who wrote a reverse harem novel about demonic bounty hunters.

It is what it is.

Eventually, if you stick with this, which some do not, you are going to reach one of two points.

You will either adjust what you write to more actively target existing, hungry markets. (Sometimes called writing to market or writing to trend, depending on how extreme it is.)

Or you will accept that writing what you want to write means either lower sales or higher advertising costs per sale.

Let me repeat again: It is not about the quality of your writing. At least not the sentence- and paragraph-level quality.

Two books could be well-written for their genre. Both could get five-star reviews. But the one that is written for a hungry market will be much, much easier to sell than the one that isn't.

Got it?

Print this out. Put it on your wall. Remember it.

Because you do not want to be comparing yourself to people who don't write what you do. The literary novelist should not be comparing sales with the romance writer. That path will lead to heartbreak.

You'll have ten sales for the month, which you're really excited about because last month you only had five, and then someone will post about how depressed they are that they only had two hundred sales this month and what a failure they are. Well, if they're a failure, what does that make you?

See how horrible that can be?

You need to remember that different genres get different results.

The easiest selling title I ever published was a billionaire romance holiday-themed short story. That thing started selling before Amazon had even told me it was live. It wasn't the quality of the writing that drove that—because I had other books that were just as well-written—it was my writing a story that readers were actively looking for. Romance, billionaire, Christmas. In 2014 that was a good combination.

Think of each title you write as creating a window of possibilities. Our literary novel about middle-age has a window of 0 to 100. A billionaire romance has a window of 50 to 1 million. (50 because there are a certain number of readers in that genre who will give any book a chance.)

What you write determines the size of your window. How well you write it determines whether you're at the top of that range or the bottom.

If you're in this to make as much money as possible,

find the largest, hottest, most voracious market you can, study the hell out of it, and then mimic what's already doing well. Don't get original. Don't be different. Give that market more of what it wants.

That's self-publishing. Feed the readers what they want, which is more of the same with maybe a slight twist.

Trade publishing, I suspect, is different.

First, it works on a longer time scale. If you get an agent today it might take another year to get a publishing contract. (Or not, remember that rock at the top of the hill analogy. I have heard of books going out on submission and selling immediately, but that's not the norm.)

Once you have that publishing contract it's very likely to be at least another year and maybe as many as three (most likely two) before your book is actually published. So all that advice that works for self-publishing about feeding a hungry market more of what it wants, goes out the window.

Three years from now, who knows what the market will be hungering for.

And your buyers are different. If you self-publish, and we'll talk about this more later, your buyers are your readers. If you trade publish, your buyers are agents and publishers. That's who you have to sell on your book.

(And let me just throw a statement in here for the technical purists that when I say "sell" I am using it to mean convince, because agents do not buy your book and publishers should actually be licensing the rights to publish the book not buying it. So you need to sell them on representing and licensing your book, respectively.)

What agents and publishers want is something they don't already have. They don't want comfort food. Yes, ultimately they're going to sell that book to readers who do, but they're trying to figure out what readers will want two or three years from now, not what they want today.

A good agent can receive over 30,000 queries in a year. How does your book stand out from the other 29,999 queries that agent is going to review this year? What makes you unique?

Agents and publishers generally do not want more of the same. If your fantasy novel is all elves and dwarves and the ultimate fight against evil, that's the same as five thousand other novels they've seen this year. So why pick you? What is special about your book?

If you want to pursue trade publishing, you need to stand out.

But not too much.

If you had to walk through a bookstore, is there a section of that store where your book would fit? What shelf should it be on? You don't get to choose ten shelves. It has to be on one. Does it fit on one? If not, even if the agent and editor love the story, you may not get a contract offer because marketing can't sell it.

(This is a lesson that also hits home when you self-publish. Because when you self-publish you have to put your book on the virtual shelves at Amazon. And you soon realize how tricky that can be. My YA fantasy is not really an epic fantasy or sword & sorcery. So where the heck does it go? That's what the marketing department is going to ask about your book. Where can we put this book to find readers who will buy it?)

The other challenge you run into on the trade side is that it's limited. Each publisher can only publish so many books per year. There are only so many slots available.

If you write a novel that has ten potential publishers who have a total of 1,000 slots available you are more likely to sell that book than if you write a novel that has two potential publishers with 100 slots available between them.

And those publishers are all going to be thinking about how many copies that book will sell. It could be brilliant, but if they think it will only sell 500 copies they'll probably choose the almost brilliant submission they have that will sell 5,000 copies.

So you need to be unique and different, but not so unique and different that you can't fit neatly on the shelves.

I will say that I think this changes as you become an established author. There is leeway in terms of what you write and how cleanly it fits between the lines once you have an established fan base. I have authors I will read no matter what. Juliet Marillier is one of them. She's yet to let me down so I don't even read what her books are about, I just buy them.

But as a new writer, no matter which path you take, you don't have reader trust yet. So you need to think about delivering what your buyers want (agents/editors for trade, readers for self) and making it as easy and seamless as possible for them to say yes.

What you choose to write and how easily it will sell determines everything else, no matter which path you take.

Alright. Now let's continue this discussion with reader expectations.

YOU NEED TO CONSIDER READER EXPECTATIONS

Now that you understand how important what you choose to write is, let's talk about reader expectations and genre. It's surprising how often this conversation occurs on the self-publishing forums I frequent.

Usually it comes up with respect to romance. Someone will come in and say "Romances don't have to end with the couple together do they?" Or "I wrote this really cool action-packed adventure novel where the two characters have a really passionate sex scene before killing all the bad guys. I can call that a romance, can't I?"

What these questions show is a lack of understanding of reader expectations and genre.

If you ever find yourself thinking, "I could write that type of book better because I wouldn't include X like every other book in that genre does," you need to step back from your keyboard.

Readers read what they do because they want a specific emotional experience.

Romance readers want to follow the journey of how

two people come together. They don't care how bad it gets in between, but they expect those two people to work it out, get past their issues, and get together. That journey should be the focus of the novel.

Two people having sex is not a romance.

It's the emotional journey that matters. Sex or no sex is not what defines romance.

Other genres have their expectations, too.

I like to read coming of age fantasy. I expect there to be magical elements in the story, because it's a fantasy, and I expect a young character who goes through some sort of growth arc that involves learning more about the world and themselves. I also expect that things will turn out well in the end. That our hero will win.

Call something coming of age fantasy and then have it end with the destruction of our young hero and I'm not going to read you again. Call that dark fantasy, however, and you're fine.

You can write whatever you want. You can even call it whatever you want. But if you want to actually sell what you've written then you better pay attention to reader expectations and how to meet them.

Which brings us back to that, "I'll do what no one else in this genre does," line of thought that happens to the best of us.

Chances are when you think this it's because you don't understand the genre. You don't see what readers see. You think, "Another tough chick who finds out she has magical powers and falls for a demon lord, yawn." A reader thinks, "Yay, another tough chick who falls for a demon lord. I love those kinds of stories."

So when you write some wimpy girl who can't do anything for herself and falls for the librarian, you are not writing books for that audience. Now, you could get lucky. There could be an audience for wimpy girl and librarian urban fantasy. But it isn't likely to be the audience that exists for tough girl and demon lord urban fantasy.

Tropes do get old. Audiences do finally get tired of reading the same old, same old over and over again. But they tend to move from bad-boy bikers to bad-boy MMA fighters to bad-boy tattoo artists instead of from bad-boy bikers to soft-hearted cowboys.

So any time you are tempted to take a right turn from what everyone else is writing, realize that you probably won't take that audience with you. And some audiences, like the romance audience, will react quite poorly to your attempts to subvert the core of what they want.

How do you figure this out? How do you learn what a genre requires?

Well, you read. Read books in the genre and read the reviews of those books.

What did people like? What did they hate? What are the common themes?

And don't let yourself be distracted by the outliers. I can think of a successful romance that had the main hero die before the end of the book. And another that had the love interest in the first book turn into the killer in the second book. But I know about these books because people still passionately talk about it years later and not in a flattering way.

And I'd argue that the only reason those authors got

away with it was because they were so successful and well-known already that they could take that risk.

That's not you.

Give readers what they want. You can put your own spin on it. We all do. But make sure you're hitting the core of that genre.

WHO YOU'RE SELLING TO

This is one of those topics that's more focused on the self-publishers than the trade publishers, but it's important enough that I think it needed to stay in the book.

In this context when I talk about trade publishers, I'm going to be talking about the bigger ones. The Big 5 (or however many there are now).

I want to walk through how that process works at a very high level and contrast that with self-publishing, because there are some important assumptions that come into play that can be harmful if you go down the self-publishing path and take a trade publishing mindset with you.

So on the trade publishing side, you get an agent. That agent helps you get a publisher. That publisher publishes your book. If you're lucky enough, your book is made available in print, ebook, and audio formats and through a network of bookstores and libraries.

While individual readers will find your books online, say through Amazon, the focus of most advertising on the trade publishing side is on the bookstores and the libraries. If the publisher can convince Barnes & Noble to stock your book on their shelves then hopefully the reader purchases will flow from there.

As a reader, I love to walk through a bookstore and peruse the shelves to find a new-to-me author or new-to-me book. Other than referrals from people I trust, this is how I find most of the books I read.

Now stop and think about that for a second.

There are a lot of books released each year. More than can fit on the shelves at your local bookstore. So which ones end up on the shelves where someone like me can discover them?

The ones that the bookstore chooses to buy. So before the customer can discover your book, someone has to have sold the bookstore on carrying that book in the first place.

Same thing happens with the local library. Which books end up on the shelves there? The ones the library chose to buy.

Now, a trade published author can have some influence on this by developing a fan base who asks the store or the library to carry their books. Enough of your fans ask for your books, the bookstore or the library will start carrying them.

But what is more likely to happen is that someone at your publisher will talk to the buyer for that bookstore chain and convince them to stock your book long before any of your fans are even asking for that book.

There might not even be a conversation. There are catalogs that publishers send to the bookstores that the bookstores then use to pick the books they'll buy. The placement of a book in that catalog gives an indication to the bookstore about which books the publisher is pushing and those are the ones the bookstore is most likely to buy.

To help drive sales of a book on the trade side, publishers will get reviews of that book in key publications. *Industry* publications. A starred Kirkus review, for example, is very valuable. It's a big deal.

On the trade publishing side.

Do you, as an uninformed reader, know about Kirkus? Do you read the New York Times Book Review and use it to buy books? (Even if you said yes, most readers would answer no.)

Your average reader is going to listen to their Aunt Marge who says your book is fabulous before they're going to care about what Kirkus or the New York Times thought.

But for trade publishing having those reviews can mean higher orders from the bookstores and libraries, the ones driving that organic discoverability that comes from someone browsing the shelves.

So they matter. On the trade side.

So do book signings. I've heard more than one author tell a story about how they did an early book signing where no one showed or they spent most of the time giving directions to the bathroom, but how they were so well liked by that bookstore for how they handled it that that store ordered and promoted their books for them for the next decade of their career.

On the self-publishing side it's different.

Most self-publishers will list their books on various

retail sites. Amazon, Kobo, Nook, Google. It's pretty rare to have your books in a bookstore if you're self-published. Sure, there were the Amazon stores and Barnes & Noble had a deal where if you were selling enough copies through them they'd do store placement, too. And some authors who've crossed over from trade publishing to self-publishing do get regular bookstore orders.

But I'd say 98% of all self-publishing sales are direct to a customer through a retail site or hand-sold by the author at something like a science fiction convention.

This means that if you're going to self-publish you need to focus your marketing efforts on reaching readers directly. It doesn't do you much good to be a model guest at a book signing if your books aren't set up for bookstore ordering. (Which is a whole other discussion we're not going to have here.)

And that Kirkus review? A waste of money. Remember, Aunt Marge knows nothing about them.

(I use them as an example because as of today they are charging $425 to review self-published books. You can do a lot with $425 that will be far better for generating sales.)

If you're going to self-publish don't get suckered because you're still in a trade publishing mindset.

As a self-publisher you need to choose advertising options that reach the ultimate customer, your reader. That's why 99 cent and free promos are so prevalent in self-publishing. But there are other options like CPC ads, too. (Those are ads where you pay each time someone clicks on the ad. Facebook ads are one example. AMS are another and I'm a huge advocate of them because they appear on book pages on Amazon which means you are right there in front of the reader when they're ready to spend money on books.)

Now, is it really as clean-cut as I just made it sound?

No.

Trade-published authors should also be working to connect with readers. That's what blogs and Twitter and FB groups are all about.

And it is nice as a self-published author to have independent third-parties review your book. I have a couple on my first-in-series fantasy novel and they do help. But I didn't pay $400 for them. (One was free through participating in the Self-Publishing Fantasy Blog Off and one was through a Writer's Digest contest that was only $99 and gave me a chance at winning money.)

There is definitely a different focus depending on which path you take and you need to know that, especially on the self-publishing side where you're the one choosing where to spend advertising dollars. I have seen far too many new authors spend thousands to promote a self-published book and see no return for it because all of that money was spent on the types of advertising that work better for trade publishing than self-publishing.

As a self-publisher if your advertising dollars aren't getting your book in front of readers, think twice about spending that money.

WHAT YOU'RE MOST LIKELY TO SELL

Another way that trade publishing and self-publishing differ is in terms of what format you're most likely to sell.

Most new authors when they think about publishing their book think about print books. Something tangible that they can hold in their hands, sign for fans, and give to their grandma.

Now, even on the trade published side that's not a given anymore. But let's pretend that side of the business isn't as complicated as it really is, and let's focus on the big publishers who are still doing print runs for their titles.

If you go the trade publishing route, it is likely your book will be published in some form of paperback and also in ebook. Hard cover is not guaranteed. And mass market paperback seems to be in decline. (Which saddens me greatly because that's how I discover new authors and I don't like ebooks. Seems I'll be renewing my library membership soon.)

For those of you unfamiliar with the terms I just used…

If you go to a bookstore you'll see three main types of books: mass market paperbacks, trade paperbacks, and hard covers. Mass market paperbacks are the small ones that are about the size of your hand. Trade paperbacks are the paperbacks that are taller (usually 8-9 inches) and usually printed on a better type of paper. And hard covers are the ones with the pretty dust jackets and hard cover.

Often people get confused about the difference between mass market and trade paperbacks. (If you self-publish you are likely publishing a trade paperback size, so price accordingly. Somewhere in the range from $12.95 to $17.95 USD.)

Based on an article from Publisher's Weekly dated April 28, 2017, the breakdown between the different formats in 2016 for trade publishers was 24% hard cover, 46% trade paperback, 7% mass market paperback, and 22% ebook.

That means 77% of trade published books were sold in some form of print version. (We're ignoring audio which wasn't covered by that article.) So print is still very much a part of the market on the trade publishing side. (Maybe not for all authors, but overall.)

Now, on the self-publishing side, it's very different. Most self-published books sell predominantly in ebook, especially when it comes to genre fiction. For my contemporary romance novels, 99% of my sales are in ebook. For my YA fantasy novels, 95% of my sales are in ebook. And that's a pretty typical result.

That means less than 5% of my fiction sales are in paperback. So remember how we started this chapter with the fact that most new writers think about print first? That's a mistake if you're going to self-publish.

If you choose to self-publish you need to focus on ebook sales first. If you only do a print version of your book, which is the natural inclination, you will be missing out on the majority of your sales.

Now, there are some areas even with self-publishing where print is more dominant. For me that's in non-fiction. For others it's in children's books.

But even there, ebook matters more than you'd think it should.

I have some guides to Microsoft Excel that contain a number of screenshots. You would think that if any type of book would sell in print, it would be a non-fiction title with lots of images. And those guides do sell substantially more copies in print than my fiction does, but even there 44% of my sales are still in ebook.

Also, you need to understand what type of print book we're talking about. With a large trade publisher they're usually going to do a print run of X books based upon pre-orders and bookstore orders. So let's say 1,000 books that the publisher pays a printer to print up front. That money is spent, those books exist whether they sell or not.

In contrast, most self-publishers use print-on-demand (POD) services instead like KDP Print or IngramSpark. With POD the book is only printed after a customer orders the book. There is no inventory to keep and no up-front cost.

A lot of authors who move to the self-publishing side don't know that POD options exist and they start looking around for a printer. Don't do that. You'll end up with a garage full of books you can't sell.

POD is your friend. You may not have the same margins with POD as you would with a print run, but you also won't spend a ton of money on books that you then can't sell.

So to sum it up. With trade pub, think print as much as ebook. With self-pub think ebook first and only do print as POD at least initially.

NUMBERS CAN LIE

Let's start this conversation with the apples to oranges issue.

Those who advocate for self-publishing will often talk about how great it is that as a self-publisher you can get 70% of the list price of the book. So if I sell a book at $4.99 I presumably get $3.50. (Amazon charges delivery charges, so with image-heavy books that's not always the case.)

The same advocates of self-publishing point to the payout percentages on the trade publishing side and say, "Look at all that money you're giving up. You get 10% of your hardcover list price, 6% of your paperback, and 30% of your ebook. And then you have to pay an agent 15%. While I get 70%. You're a fool to give away that much money."

The main critique of this comparison is that a trade published author doesn't have to pay for their book production costs. (If you do and you aren't self-publishing, you are very likely dealing with a bad publisher and need to get out of there.)

So the argument is that, yes, the trade publishing payout percentages are lower, but a self-publisher is paying for editing, covers, and advertising out of that 70%. (And it's actually 35% if you're not in the $2.99-$9.99 range on Amazon.)

Whereas, presumably, a trade published author is not paying for any of these things. (Although I know many who do pay for things like book swag, promoting their FB or Twitter page, and their own book tours.)

The bigger difference though, which is not discussed as often, is that trade publishing is actually on a completely different payment model. At least when advances are being paid.

So I can look at some book and say, "Gee, that book only sold 1,000 copies and at $9.99 and you had 30% payout, then you only earned $3,000. That sucks."

And that author can, rightly, laugh and tell me that, no, they were paid a $10,000 advance. That's where the bulk of the money is paid on the trade side. Now, ideally, an author earns out their advance and eventually starts receiving royalty checks on top of that advance, but many never do. That advance is what they earn. And that advance is more than the payout percent times number of units sold times price. (Or else they'd have earned out their advance and be getting royalty payments.)

If you don't know the advance someone was paid for their book, you don't know what they've made on that book. Not to mention those percentages I gave above are not set in stone. You would have to see someone's contract and sales numbers to really know what they'd earned on a book.

So you can't really compare self-pub to trade pub numbers that easily. Not with what's publicly available.

Now let's talk about how numbers can lie.

One of the things people like to brag about on the trade publishing side is the number of print runs a book has had. You'll see someone say, "We're going back for our fifth printing!"

Which does mean that the book did better than expected. The key there, though, is what was expected.

Which is the more successful book: the one with one print run of 50,000 copies that sells 49,000 copies or the one with five print runs totaling 5,000 books that sells 4,900 copies?

Of course, this gets back to not comparing yourself to people who don't write what you write. Not every genre commands a 50,000-book print run. Right?

And on the trade side there's an issue with meeting your publisher's expectations. So the one that had five print runs is probably exceeding expectations where the one with one print run isn't. But in terms of sheer numbers sold and money earned the one print run author made more.

Now let's turn our attention to the self-publishing side of things. The first big issue with talking numbers in self-publishing is that a lot of the time people want to talk about how many copies they've sold or how much they've made.

And that's fine. I get it. Those are the exciting numbers.

But which is more impressive, selling 10,000 copies at 99 cents or 1,000 copies at $7.99?

I know which one I'd rather have. If I sell 1,000 copies at $7.99 I make somewhere around $5,500. If I sell 10,000 copies at 99 cents I make around $3,500. And the customers who are willing to pay $7.99 are probably much more loyal to me than the ones who only paid 99 cents.

But 10,000 sure sounds more impressive than 1,000.

So you have to be careful when you hear those numbers. (And with some you have to check to make sure they didn't include books they gave away for free, although I think that isn't as common as it once was.)

Also, and this is changing now, but a lot of self-publishers will talk about the gross amount they've made and won't include expenses. They'll say "I've made six-figures self-publishing."

(And it's a weird number they're using because it's almost always the amount they received after the distributors took their cut. So it's not even really gross earnings, it's cash-in-hand.)

What gets left out of that number is promotional costs and production costs. I had two series that grossed almost the exact same amount, but one was still in the red because of production costs while the other was very much in the black. If I just talked about how much I'd made you wouldn't know that.

There are some people who make $10,000 a month but spend $9,500 to get there. It sounds really great to make $10,000 a month. $500 a month, not so much.

So when people tell you how they're doing, if they

don't tell you the net after promotion—and to a lesser extent production—they're really not telling you anything you can judge by.

Now, lest anyone think I'm throwing shade at anyone who has good numbers, I'm not. Anyone who has sold a million copies of their books has done something worth noting whether that was at 99 cents or $9.99.

All I'm saying is that if you want to compare numbers between authors or emulate what an author did to achieve success, you need to see the whole picture. I'd much rather take the path that will make me a living wage than the one that will sell me a lot of copies but not pay my utility bill.

I'll throw another one out there while we're at it: Number of titles published.

At the beginning of this book I mentioned how many titles I've published. It seems impressive, right? Over a hundred titles.

Well, it is and it isn't, because a lot of those titles are short stories or shorter non-fiction. It's not like I've written a hundred novels. (There are some self-publishers who have. *That* is impressive.)

Many people fail to realize that with self-publishing you can publish anything. Long, short, it doesn't matter. So they come to self-publishing with a mindset of only thinking about novels and not thinking about shorter works.

Once again, details matter. If you want to ask "How many titles did you publish before you made X?" that's not a good question to ask with self-publishing, because a title could be a 2,000-word short story or a 250,000-word epic fantasy. And those two will perform very differently from one another in terms of sales.

Which brings me to a final point about numbers. Always be leery about the surveys that come out of the self-publishing world.

I write under eight pen names and have a variety of titles under each, but I have yet to see a survey that acknowledges that nuance. They all ask how many titles you've published this year and how much you spent on advertising, for example, without giving an opportunity to break that down by pen name.

I have some pen names I barely advertise. Others I advertise heavily. Some have no new releases in a year, others do. If I just answer as me and don't split all that out, it gives a false picture because each pen name operates separate from the others. They don't feed each other. If I publish four books in a year under one name and in one series that will have different results than publishing four books in a year under four different names.

People mean well. But most of the surveys I've seen are not done well. So I don't participate in them anymore.

Which is not to say that the numbers you see are lies. You can do very, very well in self-publishing. There are authors who make six-figures a month self-publishing. Not many. But they do exist. There are even more authors who make six-figures a year self-publishing.

The caution I am giving here is to not trust the data on what it took to get there. Genre matters. Writing in a series matters. Frequency of release matters. Price point matters. Promotion matters. Networking matters. I have yet to see a survey that adequately accounts for all of it.

So numbers are good. You just need to understand what the numbers are actually telling you. On either the trade or self-publishing sides.

(And I should add that on the trade side, because of the ability of bookstores to later return books, that number of units initially sold may have nothing to do with number of units ultimately sold.)

Okay. Onward.

YOUR CAREER WILL NOT BE MADE WITH ONE BOOK

Hard truth time. Remember that book you spent years writing? That you love more than anything else in your life? (Or perhaps hate because you've spent so much time with it.)

If you want to make a career out of this, you will need to write another book. And another one after that. And another one after that.

It is very, very rare to be able to make an entire career out of a single book. Often writers don't even take off until they've published the third, fourth, or fifth book in a series.

Let me give you an example I've witnessed personally, George RR Martin.

I was working at a bookstore when the first Game of Thrones book was published. (I even had an ARC of it at one point.)

But it wasn't a big deal at the time. Didn't even register for me as a bookstore employee. Game of Thrones, what?

I'm sure we sold copies. But it wasn't any sort of phenomenon at the time that the first book in the series released.

If it had been I would've remembered us stocking it at the front of the store or customers coming in and asking for it. Didn't happen.

It took continuing to write that series and slowly build a fan base before those books really broke out. And I would argue it was actually the TV series that was the turning point.

It wasn't like people picked up book 1 and said, "This is genius. It's the best book I've ever read. Give me more."

Could George RR Martin live happily ever after on the sales of book 1 of the series now? Maybe. But it took writing more in the series for that to happen.

Because step back and think about what it would mean and what it would take for one single book to support you financially forever. (Assuming that's your goal.)

I'll do this with self-publishing numbers because they're easier.

Let's say you want to receive a check for $40,000 from your writing each year. And that you can price that book at $4.99, so you're getting $3.50 for each sale.

To receive $40,000 you would need to sell about 11,500 copies of that book every single year for the next fifty years. Is that likely? No.

Not on either path. Especially if there's nothing for readers to go to after that first book. They might like you just fine, but they already read your book so they're on to the next.

Many self-published authors, and I assume trade published as well, make the fatal mistake of trying to promote or fix their first book. Either because the book does really well so they keep trying to get more sales, or because the book doesn't do well and they think they need to re-write it, put new covers on it, or "fix it" in some other way.

But if you focus on that first book and never publish anything else, what do you think happens to the readers who did buy your book and like it?

You lose them.

They go read someone else. If you're lucky they'll be there when you finally publish again. But most of us aren't that lucky. For most of us, someone will read our book, enjoy it just fine, even be willing to buy something more from us, but they'll move on if we don't have more to give them. And they won't come back.

So if you want this to be a career, you either need to be so phenomenal that readers will wait for years for you (don't count on that one) and recommend your books to everyone they know so that the books keep selling, or you need to be able to write more books.

Trade publishing seems to be set for releases of one book per year per series. Some authors might juggle two series so they have two releases per year (Mercedes Lackey comes to mind), but one per year per series seems to be the norm. A few authors get away with being slower, but all you have to do is look at comments from George RR Martin's fans or Patrick Rothfuss's fans to see how unhappy fans get when an author they like isn't producing fast enough.

(And those are the lucky authors who have fans that care instead of move on.)

With self-publishing, it's best to write even faster than that. I'd say ideally four novels a year. (Note that I do not do this for any of my pen names. I'm also not a six-figure author, so put those two together. But we'll talk about this more later, the fact that there are different paths to success.)

Good news is that the more novels you write, the less time it will probably take you to write each one. My first fantasy novel took 450 hours to write. My second fantasy novel took 215 hours.

It's not guaranteed it will happen that way—we all make the mistake of tackling a novel we're not yet ready to write at one point or another—but it's likely that as you do this more you will get better at it and at knowing what works for you.

I will suggest that if you're at that stage where it took you seven years to write your first novel and your dream is to do this full-time, you should start working on that next novel immediately. You don't want to get your shot, put out a book readers love, and then lose them because you can't follow it up fast enough.

There's another point to be made here. And it's an important one.

Because your career will not be built on just one novel, don't let the failure of one novel stop you.

So that novel didn't sell? So what? Write the next one.

Easier said than done, I know.

But if you realize that a career as a writer could involve writing forty novels or even more—some self-publishers write a dozen a year—then you start to see that the failure of one of those novels is just a setback not an ending.

Now, you can take the decade-a-novel approach. No one is saying you can't. I'm just saying that it will be that much harder to make a living at writing if you do.

Which means it's a good time to talk about how there is not one path to take with this writing thing.

THERE ISN'T ONE PATH

Throughout this book I've been talking about trade publishing and self-publishing. In my view those are two separate paths to the same ultimate goal: being paid for your writing. And in my opinion one is not inherently better than the other. (I know. Others disagree. On both sides.)

As I mentioned at the start, I am self-published. It's because I am an inpatient person. When you tell me I have to wait a year to hear back from an agent to see if they want my novel and then another year to hear back from publishers and then two more years until that book is out, I lose interest. I can do a lot in four years and by the time that book is out I'll have forgotten it even exists.

I also like to write what I write when I write it and how I want to write it. Having someone dictate what I can write and when I should write it is not something that works for me.

Self-publishing is a good fit for me because of that. I

can write a book, edit it, and publish it the next week. (And then move on to the next and no one will care.)

But self-publishing is not for everyone. As much as things have improved over the years there is still a substantial amount of disdain towards self-publishers. One of self-publishing's greatest strengths—that anyone can publish anything—is also its greatest weakness.

If you value the recognition of and validation from your peers, trade publishing is still the way to go. I tend not to care what anyone thinks of me and I still notice some of that kickback when I talk to other writers. It's not pleasant.

Also, if you want to walk into a bookstore and take a picture of your book on the shelves, chances are you need to be trade published for that.

And if you're a very collaborative personality who enjoys working with others, then trade publishing is also still probably the better path.

Self-publishing can be lonely. You're out there all alone making big decisions with no one to lend their insight or experience. It's daunting. Rewarding for those it works for, but demoralizing for those it doesn't work for.

When people think about publishing these days those are the two main distinctions they think about, but there is another division I want to talk about that comes up especially within self-publishing. And that's the fast release/hit the charts approach versus the slow release/rank doesn't matter approach.

Either path can work. I know six-figure authors who release once a month, but I also know six-figure authors who release once a year.

I bring this up because I was at a conference recently where someone on a panel stated that the only way to be successful at self-publishing was to do rapid releases. A book a month. And that if you didn't do that you couldn't possibly succeed at self-publishing. (This person was not self-published, by the way.)

Now, I will give a nod to that statement.

The most sure-fire way to succeed at self-publishing is to publish frequently, in a hot market, and in a series that follows a core group of characters that your readers love.

Hot market means lots of potential sales. Core group of characters that readers love means reader loyalty and guaranteed sales of each release. Publishing frequently means that readers don't forget about you.

But not all of us can do that. Or want to do that.

I can write fast. Not a novel a month, but I could easily do four novels a year and probably six if I really wanted to.

What I can't do is write the same thing over and over again. Or write to a hungry market. I tried. I wrote that billionaire romance. And it did far better than anything else I'd written at that point. But I just didn't have it in me to keep writing that. Some people do. Some people are happy to write whatever they need to write to make money.

Others are not.

I have eight pen names. I write romance, mystery, fantasy, and a wide, wide variety of non-fiction from dating to puppies to Microsoft Excel. That is who I am. So I have had to accept that the path I am on is a slower path.

But it's not a dead-end path.

Each year of the last eight years (knock wood that this continues) I have made more than the year before to the point that I now am making enough from this to support myself if I were willing to live somewhere cheap and cut back on luxuries.

I know other authors who publish slowly who are making far more than I am. There is not one path to success either on the self or the trade publishing side.

You need to look inside and understand who you are as a writer. Know what you can do and what you can't. And then listen to the people who are like you. See how those people have succeeded.

I know for a fact that if I had to commit to writing twelve reverse harem novellas this year that I would probably not finish one of them. But if I just tell myself, "Sit down and write whatever you want. The only condition is you finish what you start" that I'll put out a good 350K words of new material and that one of those books I publish might take off.

Don't let the path others have taken distract you from yours. Sure, listen if it works for you. Try it if you're unhappy with how you're doing. But accept that what others do might not work for you or might make you miserably unhappy and that it may take you longer to get there but it's still doable.

This is especially true on the self-publishing side where even the readers put pressure on authors to produce more and more, faster and faster. (I forget who but there was a romance author a while back who shared an email from a fan that basically said, "I don't care that your husband is dying, if you don't publish a book a month I'll stop reading you." Seriously? No.)

You have to be grounded in who you are to survive all the varying pressures you're going to face as a writer. Keep your head down and you be you.

Now, following on this, let's talk about a question that comes up far more than it should. The question is, "When should I quit trying to trade publish and self-publish instead?"

WHEN TO QUIT TRYING TO TRADE PUBLISH

I often hear people ask, "When should I quit trying to get my book trade published and self-publish it instead?"

The answer to this question is simple.

Never.

This belief that self-publishing is what you do when you fail at trade publishing is still very prevalent. It came up at a conference I was just at and was asked by two separate people in the audience.

First, let me say that that attitude is incredibly insulting to anyone who has chosen to self-publish. Behind it is this attitude that, "Oh, you couldn't hack it the real way, so you just had to settle for this."

And I get it. There are people who have "given up" on trade publishing and self-published. Heck, I sort of started that way. I had short stories that almost sold to pro-paying markets (darn you Tor.com) and rather than move on to the semi-pro or token markets, I self-published those stories instead. I figured I could make more that way.

(Haha. I was wrong. I learned.)

So I understand where this attitude comes from. But it's a foolish way to think of things. Here's why.

As a self-publisher I not only have to know how to tell an engaging story or write an informative easy-to-read non-fiction title (which is the same thing you need to do to get an agent or publisher), but I also have to handle all other aspects of production and marketing.

It doesn't matter if you're going to pay someone else to do it or do it yourself, you should still know what it takes to create a quality product and to sell that product.

Ask yourself:

Would you know if that person you just hired to edit your book is a good editor? How?

(Many self-publishers have found that the person they hired to edit their book was not qualified only when the bad reviews rolled in.)

What about your cover? Do you know what kind of cover you need so that your readers will know this is the book for them?

It isn't just about having a pretty cover. It's about having an *appropriate* cover. There's a reason so many romance novels have naked man chest on them.

Now you can hire a cover designer, but most will look to you for direction. You are the one who will need to know when something isn't working. And you'll need to be able to tell that to your cover designer, which is easier said than done.

What about colors. Do you know what colors work for your genre? Do they use blues and purples? Reds?

Yellows? Black and white with a dash of color? (It matters.)

And are the covers in your genre photo manipulations or illustrated? What fonts are being used? Are they serif or non-serif fonts?

And what about the blurb? The description of your story. Can you write appealing back cover copy? Or can you recognize appealing back cover copy if you pay someone else to write it?

(This is one of my personal weak spots. I took 90,000 words to tell that story and now I have to boil it down to an enticing three paragraphs? Hahaha. You're kidding, right?)

And then what about categories? Where do you list your book? Do you actually know what you've written? (Hint: It's not a romance if one of the people dies before the end of the book. And it's not chick lit if it's dark and gritty.)

Do you know the difference between non-fiction and fiction? (You think I'm kidding, but I'm not.)

And then there's advertising.

Let's assume you wrote a book that people will enjoy, that it has the right cover for the genre, and a strong blurb. Now how do you find your readers? Where are they? How do you reach them?

If you self-publish, it's unlikely that you're going to be in physical bookstores. (Despite what some will say, that's just not a common outcome for most self-publishers.)

So how do you rise above everyone else online to get your perfect cover in front of your perfect reader? I just went to Amazon and chose book releases in the last 90 days. Do you know how many titles there were? 70,000.

How are you going to get your book in front of readers when you're competing against 70,000 other new releases plus the millions of books that are already out there?

As a self-publisher you will need to be able to do everything I just mentioned if you want to be successful. (Sure. You can throw any old book up on Amazon with any cover you please, no editing, a horrible description, bad categories, and no ads. Just don't expect it to sell. In which case, why did you bother? Better to spend that money and time in Vegas.)

(And again, I've been there myself. I have thrown that book up on Amazon and I have had the lack of sales that went with that approach. So I'm not knocking anyone who does that. I'm just saying that it's not going to get you anywhere, so why do it.)

Now, let's contrast what I just covered with the trade publishing path. If you want to trade publish all you need to do to get paid money for your book is write a good enough book and a good enough query to sell that book to a publisher. (I'm assuming here you're selling it to a publisher who pays an advance.)

Once you sell that small handful of people (agent, editor, acquisitions board) with the potential of your story, someone else will do the cover and hire the editor. And, sure, you'll probably have to do some promotion, but your agent and publisher will be right there working with you on what to do, not to mention doing their part to get bookstore placement for you and industry reviews.

Of the two paths, self-publishing requires mastery of far more skills than the trade publishing path does. Failing at a path that requires you to master skill A and then deciding to take a path that requires you to master skills A, B, C, D, and E is not going to turn out well.

It's like saying "I couldn't complete the half-marathon, so I decided to do a triathlon instead."

That may work for 1 in a million personalities, but it isn't going to work for most.

Now, don't get me wrong. There are reasons to self-publish. Timing, control, and more potential profit are the three that come immediately to mind. Flexibility is another. I self-published my first non-fiction title because I had something I wanted to say and knew I couldn't get it trade published.

But if you think of self-publishing as what you do when you give up, then you are going to fail there, too.

So let me give you this advice:

Rather than self-publish, write another book.

Actually, write three more books.

Novels. Write three more novel-length works.

Do not rewrite the same book over and over again. Write new material. Ideally in a new setting with new characters. You can stay in the same story world if you want, but brand new people with brand new problems.

And pay attention to your market while you're doing this. Read a ton in the area where you want to publish so you can understand what readers want and what they're already getting.

Write. Read. Write. Read. Write some more.

And query those novels. Keep following the trade

publishing path. Keep trying to get an agent, because that's what you want, right? That's your Plan A.

Chances are that if you write three more novels you will sell one of them. And congratulations. You'll be on the path you wanted to be on in the first place.

No Plan B for you. No fallback. You will have worked at the path you wanted enough to succeed at it. It is far better to take all that time and energy you would've spent learning how to be a publisher (editing, covers, blurbs, etc.) and apply it to being a better writer.

Now I'm not saying you aren't a perfectly decent writer right now. You could very well be technically proficient. Your sentences could all be just fine. But maybe you're missing the mark when it comes to genre. Or maybe the problem is there's nothing unique or new about what you've written that would appeal to an agent or publisher.

If you give it four tries—the novel that already failed plus three more—you are going to be able to narrow in on that goal.

And if by then you've figured out that trade publishing isn't for you, you will be much better positioned to succeed at self-publishing. You will know more about the market. You will have more material to publish which increases the odds of readers finding you. And you'll have a better feel for who you are as a writer.

The key here is to realize that if you self-publish now, it will slow you down. You will be taking time you could devote to improving your storytelling and putting it towards learning how to publish instead. And don't even get me started on the amount of time you will lose to excessively checking your sales reports.

Self-publishing should not be your Plan B. Choose self-publishing because it's the path you want to take. And understand that if you go down that path you will be putting in a lot of time and energy on things that are not writing. (But it won't be 90% of your time, not unless you choose to do that to yourself. Another lovely wrong fact that was given out at this conference I was at.)

DON'T LET ANYONE CONTROL YOUR DREAMS

So I just went through this long and detailed discussion about why self-publishing shouldn't be your Plan B. That if you want to trade publish you should stick with it. And now I'm going to say something that may sound like I'm contradicting myself.

Which is this: Do not allow anyone else to control your ability to achieve your dreams.

If you are sitting there with a book that you love and that you want to share with the world. And if that book has been rejected by every agent and every publisher out there and you are shattered by this, because this book was a labor of love and you wanted to see it published.

If that is you, why would you let the decision of strangers dictate whether that book gets shared with the world? In this day and age, with self-publishing as a viable alternative, why would you let a small group of strangers control your dream?

I know. This is in direct contradiction to what I said above. So let me try to clarify the distinction here.

The previous chapter was for someone who wants to be a writer. They're willing to write five different novels to get there. They'll keep trying because what they want more than anything is to be published.

This chapter is for someone who has written the book of their heart and is ready to quit. They spent years getting this book right and now no one wants it. So they're going to walk away from writing. No one wants to hear the story they want to tell and it hurts them to know this.

For that writer—the one that has this *one* story that matters so much to them—I ask why not self-publish?

Now, if you want to see sales from this you're going to have to do the work. You'll have to learn all those skills I mentioned above. You'll have to study covers and learn about blurbs and about editing and everything else it takes to get that book out there looking like what you envisioned.

But if this book means that much to you, why wouldn't you do that?

I have seen writers on forums or in blog posts declare defeat. Sometimes it's been a trade-published author whose publisher doesn't want their next book, because the author took a chance and went in a new direction and the publisher doesn't think the fans will go there with them. Sometimes it's a new author who has written that one book and can't find an agent or publisher for it.

These people are sad. They put that book away in the drawer knowing no one will get to see it and feeling broken by that knowledge.

If that's how you feel, why not give that book a

chance? Why not self-publish it? Get it out into the world if it matters that much to you.

Don't give up that easy. Don't let others control your fate.

You need to decide what matters most to you. Getting that book into the hands of readers? Or doing it the "right way"?

If that book matters enough to you, you'll find a way to get it published no matter what.

LEVELS OF WRITING ABILITY

Phew. That felt intense to write, not sure if it felt intense to read. But let's step back for a bit and talk about what you might learn if you do decide to stay on the trade publishing path and write three more novels.

Some people won't learn anything. They'll just go on blindly making the same mistakes over and over again.

To do this right you need to be reading and learning about the industry while you're writing those new novels. Just writing and not paying attention to other books is not going to help you.

If you read enough and pay enough attention to what's selling, you will start to learn something about writing that most new writers don't realize. I know I didn't.

Most new writers think that writing is about what happens at the sentence level. Maybe they think it's about what happens at the paragraph level. And that does play into things. Your writing needs to be clear enough that it can convey your story.

For example, I read *How Proust Can Change Your Life* and loved it. Great book. It made me excited to read Proust, so I bought his book, too. Couldn't get past page two. The writing was so dense and convoluted that I just could not get into it at all. (And I enjoy reading Tolstoy, so it's not like I'm a lightweight when it comes to reading.)

Clearly, from *How Proust Can Change Your Life*, there were great insights in Proust's books but I never found them because I couldn't get past the writing.

So the first level of writing that all writers need to master is how to tell the story in their head in a way that others can follow.

What order do you put the words in so that it makes sense to your reader? Is it clear who "he" is referring to in that sentence? Is your reader going to be able to visualize the scene based on your description? Can they feel it? Can they taste it? Did you describe too much so that they put your book down and walked away out of boredom? Are they rolling their eyes at your character's lengthy description of how attractive she is while looking at herself in the mirror? Etc.

Most critique groups I've participated in focus on this level of writing. And they pretty much have to because they are geared towards reviewing small chunks of writing at a time.

But being a good writer is about more than that.

The next level of writing ability, in my opinion, is hitting reader expectations for your genre. If I'm reading a fantasy I want it to be a fantasy. I don't want aliens showing up in chapter 20. A romance reader wants the couple to get together. A mystery reader wants there to be a mystery that is solved by the end of the book.

If you aren't meeting reader expectations it doesn't matter how good your sentences are, readers won't come back to you.

But there are steps beyond that level.

I haven't worked out what all of them are yet. I'm still learning.

One I like to call emotional resonance. You can write perfect sentences and follow genre conventions to a T, but if you don't connect with the reader on an emotional level they probably won't be coming back to you.

Now maybe in non-fiction this isn't as necessary and maybe in hard science fiction or tough guy urban fantasy you can get away without the emotional level. But I would say that for most fiction writers your readers need to be given an emotional experience that fits with what they expect from that type of book.

I blogged about this topic recently and mentioned two books in that post that failed for me at this level. Both were well-written. Both followed fantasy conventions. But I will never read either of those authors again, because they disappointed me emotionally. They solved story problems in a way that was distasteful to me.

As you write and read and write and read and write and read, you will start to get a feel for this.

Ask yourself, why did I like that book? Why didn't I like this other one? Why is this book a hit and that other one not?

It is far too common to hear writers say, "Dan Brown

is a horrible writer," "Twilight is awful", and "I can't believe anyone would ever read Fifty Shades of Grey."

Those writers are ones who are still stuck at the beginning. They think it's about writing perfect sentences. It's not.

Your sentences only have to be good enough to convey your message. (This is why I told the grammar purists to run at the beginning of the book. Because if any are still around they are screaming right now about how wrong I am.)

All I have to say to them is, "Have you really looked at how many rules Stephen King breaks with his writing?" I love how fearless he is. He's one of the few authors I know of who puts things in parens in fiction. It is a wonder to behold.

And readers love him. They love him because he surprises them. Because he takes everything five steps further than most authors would dream of taking things. Read *Gerald's Game* if you don't believe me. Bad enough to have a woman tied to a bed in a remote cabin with her husband dead on the floor. But where he takes it? Geez.

Think about this as you write and as you read. Think about what's there in the books you like and missing in the ones you don't. Focus on the authors you read and think are okay but don't buy more of versus the authors you read and order the entire rest of the series the next day. What is the difference between them? Why choose one over the other?

It's not the sentences. Or at least not just the sentences.

If you want to be really good at this, you need to

move past the sentence-level. (And I don't have all the answers here, yet. I'm still working it out myself. I just know it's there. And that the more you read and write and analyze, the more you'll be able to see what your writing needs that it's missing right now.)

TAKING THINGS PERSONALLY

Alright, I only have two more topics to go and they don't flow easily from the last discussion. So we're just going to have to take a hard right turn here. Because I want to talk about professionalism and taking things personally.

There is a lot of rejection involved in publishing. A lot. You query agents, they ignore you. Or they send you a form letter. And you feel lucky because they sent you a form letter. You submit short stories, more rejections. You finally get an agent and they send your novel off to editors. More rejection. Or more silence.

You think it ends when you publish your first book, but it doesn't. Because then it becomes all about sales and reviews. Your publisher (or you if you self-published) expected 1,000 sales. You got 100.

You thought people would love it, but they gave it one- and two-star reviews.

Your book actually did okay, but the publisher doesn't want more from you.

Your book did well, but your agent doesn't like your next story idea and decides to drop you.

On the self-publishing side you can be running a successful promo and suddenly have someone leave a one-star review that's wrong but stops your momentum. Or you can be doing really well and then Amazon takes your page reads away and threatens to close your account.

All of this rejection can get to you. It can feel really personal. It can feel like someone has it in for you. Like it's not just how the system works for everyone, but that someone is out to get you personally. That they don't like *you* and that's why they did that.

I have seen this far too often. An author who gets a one-star review and fights back with the reviewer. Or gets rejected by an agent and posts a nasty blog post about it. Or has Amazon do something (and Amazon is always doing something) and they start sending off over-the-top, vitriol-filled emails to Jeff Bezos.

Do not do this.

It is not personal.

Agents get 30,000 queries a year. They do not have the time to make it personal. If they reject you, it's just the writing wasn't what they wanted right then. It's not *you*.

And with Amazon? It definitely isn't personal. Instead of going from fine to insanely angry, try a simple email using please and thank you and not making any sort of crazy accusations.

If you've ever worked anywhere where you had to deal with customer complaints you know that you were probably a little nicer to the people who were nice to you.

Right? So be nice even when someone has done something that upsets you.

The best advice I can give you is to keep calm, be nice, and stay professional at all times. On both the trade- and self-published side of this business there are opportunities to act inappropriately. Some have even ended in lawsuits. Don't get sucked into that. Don't go out and attack others, either your fellow writers, fans, or agents and publishers. Do not do it.

And let me remind you of one more fact: Amazon, Kobo, Google, Penguin Random House, etc., etc. are all businesses. None of them are non-profits. Which means that they make decisions that benefit their bottom line. That can impact you. It can impact you significantly. But it's never about you.

It's about making their owners happy. Even when those decisions benefit you—like Amazon creating KDP in the first place—it's not about you. If they do something that benefits you, you should expect that it benefited them more. And if they do something that harms you, you should expect they did it because that benefited them too.

It is not about you. It is about them.

Which means it is not personal. And trying to make it personal will not help you.

I know. Easier said than done. I've had those insane reviews. I've been blind-sided by that vendor that changed things overnight. I've been upset, too.

But you can't let it get to you. You have to push those feelings aside and move on from it. One, for your own mental health. And, two, because you will not survive in this business if you can't. No matter which path you take.

VISIBILITY

Okay. Last topic.

In an ideal world we'd all be able to write whatever book we wanted, put it out there into the world, and it would just sell and sell and sell. Every single reader who might love that book would find it easily and we'd all just be happy.

But that's not how it works.

Your readers end up reading books they hate and never find yours. It's an imperfect system.

You can do things to help connect with your readers, though. How?

By either making yourself or your books more visible.

For example, I went to a conference last month and there was going to be a half-day session by three authors. In anticipation of that session, I bought one book from each of them to read so that I would be able to judge their advice in context. (Remember the whole "listen to people who write what you write" advice above?)

Well, turns out I ended up buying and reading six of

the books one of those authors had written because I enjoyed them so much. (Interestingly, I know nothing about their other series but just on title alone am unlikely to read it even though I enjoyed this series. As a writer you need to be careful every time you change worlds or characters because you are very likely to lose readers.)

That's a good example of making yourself visible. This author participated on a panel which brought them to my attention which led me to buy their books.

Other authors make themselves visible through Twitter, Facebook, or Reddit; by blogging; by doing podcasts; by selling books at conventions; by participating on forums; etc.

If someone encounters you and likes you, there is a chance that they'll give your books a try. So visibility can be important. Of course, if they encounter you and don't like you, that will work against you. Someone who might have otherwise liked your book will refuse to read it.

This kind of free, organic visibility is available to any authors, trade or self-published.

Self-published authors have access to a different type of visibility, the type provided by paid advertising and discounted books. (Not to say that trade publishers don't do this, too, just that it's under the author's control when you self-publish.)

For example, today I'm running one of my romance novels free on Freebooksy. That should get me about 3,000 downloads of that title. It's like a taste test at the local grocery store. Did you like what you just tried for free? Why don't you buy some more then?

Many self-publishers use either temporary free runs or

set their first-in-series title to free to attract new readers. And there are plenty of places where you can advertise your free book to get it in front of readers who might like it. (BookBub being the king of those sites, but also one of the hardest ones to get.)

I actually prefer pay-per-click advertising instead. That's advertising that you do on Facebook or through Amazon using AMS ads, for example, where you pay each time someone clicks on your ad. On Amazon I can run those types of ads on full-price books so that I am putting my book in front of potential readers every single day.

The final way to get visibility is by selling well. Success leads to more success. When I was working at that bookstore we'd take the weekly best-seller list and discount all of the books on that list by 30% and put them on the front store display. So if someone sold well enough to get on the list in the first place they were very likely to continue to do well because stores all across the country were going to display and discount their book.

On Amazon if you do well you'll end up on the top 100 lists that readers can browse. And you'll end up featured in the emails Amazon sends to customers. And that can be a self-replicating cycle. Do well, get listed, have emails go out, get sales from those emails, stay on those lists, get more sales, and on and on and on.

Add to this the fact that Amazon also makes it easier to stay highly ranked than to become highly ranked. It does not take the same number of daily sales to stay at a certain ranking as it does to get there in the first place.

Now, whether someone finds you through social

media or through advertising or through placement of some other sort, the book still has to be good. A sale price or being likeable will get you one sale. But if the book itself isn't good, you're not going to get more sales after that.

I am of the opinion that everyone should advertise. (If you're trade published that probably means working the social media or convention circuit or bookstore tours and keeping an eye on your books so you know when they're on sale and can tell your followers. If you're self-published that means social media and price promotions.)

I know some self-publishers who claim that they don't need to advertise. That they just write such good books that people buy them without ads.

Be careful thinking that can be you. One, most people's books do not grab readers so well that they can just live on word of mouth. Two, even if you do write books like that they may not be in hungry markets that are actively looking for new authors, so you will need to put some effort into getting your book in front of readers. Three, many self-publishers with low advertising costs established themselves pre-2015 or so when things were very different. An established author whose sales are being fueled by word of mouth and success leading to more success can't be compared to a brand new author who is completely unknown.

So plan on advertising if you want to see sales.

And, really, even if your book can sell itself because it's well-written and feeding a hungry market, why not back that up with ads and do even better? Unless you're

#1 on all of Amazon (which a few self-publishers have achieved), there's still room to find more readers.

Obviously don't advertise if it costs you more than you make, but I think that most well-packaged, well-written books should have at least one form of advertising that is profitable for them. For some it'll be 99 cent sales with advertisements through targeted mailing lists. With others it'll be selling at full-price using CPC ads. Not all ads will scale. I have a book on dog parks that I can advertise profitably using AMS ads, but will probably never sell a hundred copies. It's still profitable, though.

If you have a book where no advertising works, you have to look at the book and try to figure out where it falls down. Check cover, title, blurb, and price first. But then look to genre expectations, reader experience, and quality of the writing.

Okay, back on point. You need visibility as an author. If you're trade published that likely means in-person appearances or social media. If you're self-published that can mean social media but it can also be accomplished through advertising your books.

And, remember, no amount of advertising is going to overcome a bad book. You'll get sales on book 1 if it's well-packaged and well-advertised, but that'll be it. The story is the key.

CONCLUSION

Alright, so that's it. That's what I had to say.

There's a challenge to writing any non-fiction book which is how in-depth you go. Do you give all the nuance and caveats or do you stick to the generalities? I'd say for this book, and for most beginner books I write, I've stayed mostly with the generalities and maybe given a hint of the nuance and caveats.

All of this is much more complex than I've made it seem. I could go through and double the size of this book just by writing out all the arguments I can envision people making against what I've said here.

But I think that would overwhelm a writer at the stage of development that this book is aimed at. So as you continue on I expect you will form your own opinions and they will vary some from what I've said here.

Read through my blog a little and you'll see I've done the same with advice I'm given. For example, I was at a conference earlier this year where the advice was not to advertise until your third book in your series is out. And I wrote a blog post about how I disagreed with that advice. Because when you publish a book and see no sales it can be soul-crushing. You labored over this book and now…nothing.

At the same time, the real advice should be to hold off on advertising as long as you possibly can. I figure I am a good enough writer that people will read what I have available. But I am not so good that they'll wait two years for my next book. Which means that every reader I convince to buy my books is pretty much only going to buy what I have available now. (And again, I'm simplifying some here.)

That means that if I get someone to buy my books when I have three out, they'll read three books by me. If I get them to buy my books when I have six out, they'll buy six from me. Well, if it costs the same amount to advertise when I have three books as it does to advertise when I have six, then doesn't it make sense to hold off until six?

Or eight or nine.

No one does that, though. It's ideal, but it's not going to happen.

So take the advice I've given here as a jumping off point. As something to sit with and then argue against. If you follow what I've said here, you'll be off to a good start. But as you move forward in your writing career, you are going to need to pivot and adjust to meet your own personal needs. Every writer's career is unique.

There are some generalities that are true for most, but we each need to make our own choices based on our own circumstances.

The one thing I will emphasize here is that being a

writer is a long and complex journey. If you succeed right out of the gate, congratulations, but in some ways that makes it even harder. Because starting at the top there's only one way to go. If you don't succeed right away, that's okay, too.

The only way you are going to fail at this is if you quit.

And if you do, so what? Selling your writing and having others judge it and put a value on it is not for everyone. I still haven't quite figured out why I write. I think part of it is that it hasn't been easy for me. But I feel no compelling need to write novels that other people read. I will always be a storyteller in my own head—it's how I entertain myself when I'm bored. But that doesn't mean I have to write for an audience or that I have to sell what I write. Same goes for you.

So if you're not happy with writing to make money, then don't do it.

But if that's what you want. To write stories, have people read them, and be paid for it, then the only person who can stop you from achieving that is you.

Don't quit. Don't give up. If this is what you really want, then make it happen. One way or the other.

ABOUT THE AUTHOR

M.L. Humphrey is a self-published author with too many titles and too many pen names who has hopefully learned a few things by now about what it takes to sell books.

You can reach M.L. Humphrey at mlhumphreywriter@gmail.com or at www.mlhumphrey.com